Books by Marvin Bell

These

Green-Going-to-Yellow

These
Green-Going-to-Yellow

POEMS BY

Marvin Bell

ATHENEUM

NEW YORK

1981

Grateful acknowledgment is given to the John Simon Guggenheim Memorial Foundation and the National Endowment for the Arts for fellowships which aided in the writing of these poems, and to the following periodicals in whose pages these poems previously appeared:

THE AMERICAN POETRY REVIEW: *Benny Hooper, Letters from Africa, Life, On and On, A Shrug, Someone Is Probably Dead, Tired* and *You Can Keep the Sun Out of Your Eyes with Just One Hand.*
ANTAEUS: *Haleakala Crater, Maui; The Hedgeapple, Late Naps, The Mummies of Guanajuato* and *That Time in Tangier.*
THE ANTIOCH REVIEW: *Things I Took.*
THE ATLANTIC MONTHLY: *During the War* and *The Last Thing I Say.*
CRAZYHORSE: *Cuba, Fifties;* and *In America.*
THE MISSOURI REVIEW: *At the Airport, Florence, Some Shadows, What They Do to You in Distant Places* and *Where Is Odysseus From and What Was He Before He Left for the Trojan War?*
THE NEW YORKER: *A Motor* and *These Green-Going-to-Yellow.*
PLOUGHSHARES: *Birds Who Nest in the Garage* and *The Canal at Rye.*
POETRY MISCELLANY: *We Had Seen a Pig.*
TENDRIL (*The Poet's Choice*): *He Said To.*
THE VIRGINIA QUARTERLY REVIEW: *Italian* and *To an Adolescent Weeping Willow.*
WATER TABLE: *He Said To.*

Some of these poems are dedicated, as follows: "The Hedgeapple," to James Galvin and Jorie Graham; "Haleakala Crater, Maui," to John and Mollie Geyer; "Late Naps," to Gerald Bruns and Vernon Cudgel; "Tired," to John and Nancy Morgan; "Cuba, Fifties," to Lew Carson; "On and On," to John Irving; "That Time in Tangier," to Daniel Halpern; and "At the Airport," to Larry Levis.

Library of Congress Cataloging in Publication Data

Bell, Marvin.
   These green-going-to-yellow.

   I. Title.
PS3552.E52T4 1981   811'.54   81–66013
ISBN 0–689–11228–9   AACR2
ISBN 0–689–11227–0 (pbk.)

To Harry and Kathleen

Contents

1

The Hedgeapple

1

I wish we'd gone back—
you didn't tell me she came off her porch
and ran through the green yards
waving us back as we drove away
but all the time in our blind spot.
That heavy fruit, the hedgeapple,
had made us stop. Then when she came waving
to the screen we flinched
a foot down on the gas pedal not to be
pinned for having intentions
on her hedgeapple tree.
She knew us,
she told you later,
but still we had the fear of correspondence,
and the guilt that comes from watching
someone else's treasure
in the open,
and also the fear of letting things be
more than they seem and ourselves less.
We should have gone back.

Do the trees really laugh?
Can we smell the light?
Is there smoke inside the cornstalk
and a light inside the tree,
a light that will not find where it came from?
What they call a hedgeapple—
it is one more perversion of the apple,
one more story like unto the ancient
unwilling airs and dances.
I am sure that we could have stolen one
and taken a bite apiece
and made ourselves crazy from the ground up.
We should have gone back.

We should have beckoned the wind
back into the hedgeapples
and her back in through the screen.

2

In spring, when the trees laugh,
like men and women who have been breathing
deeply and are also thirsty,
and the light
increases and increases
its waxy luxury so that a stand of bush
might seem an artist's wash,
we forget
what we were told.

First, the hedgeapple
is the giant birthing of a tree,
not a hedge, and second,
is no apple. A lemon grapefruit, maybe.
Like a grapefruit, but green.
Like an apple, but lemony.

We were lucky,
three in a car, the language we spoke
seeming to make light everywhere
because we stopped to look.
For a moment then, we forgot
what we were told.
And we didn't think.
Without us, the hedgeapple is perfect—
means nothing.
We should have gone back.
I am sure now she was watching us
from the beginning,
and the whole time too.

We thought we didn't take her hedgeapple.
We should have given it back.

So: here.

Haleakala Crater, Maui

I'm not going to reveal
the task I had, but it was big
and, as it should have been if
this is Life, beyond me.
I wanted something beyond me,
something the simple thought of which
shed night over all my reasons
and required of me more
than I required of myself,
something terrible, for one might talk
about it only to a lode of black
Godliness, such as one might come to
next to the blowhole of a volcano,
or take it unsaid to the psychical core-magnet
risen from lava and sulfur,
shepherd of cinder cone and crater,
sure in a hole in the clouds,
bottomless and wind-drawn,
mortal god immortal to men, there.
I walked. Or did not walk
but fought forward, wind-driven-back,
to take from that density
strength for a hard job coming.
It wasn't perfection I wanted,
with its need for form, hollow
unbroken shell, for all we know.
A place like this is different.
This is way beyond the social precepts
for which men have been flayed and women
turned inside out and flung down.
This is rock, massive, shocking,
lording over a green benevolence of fields,
unpromising, but absolutely
to be there.
Whoever has yet to be born

will understand me when I say that
I was once in a whistle
and I was once in a fish.
And I was once in the center of the earth.
These were experience "beyond." And beyond these?
Beyond these is this heaviness
of the inner organs of a whole planet
spit-up to stay, powerfully
corresponding to our hard, twisted gut-ropes.

Life

I leave the office, take the stairs,
in time to mail a letter
before 3 in the afternoon—the last dispatch.
The red, white and blue air mail
falls past the slot for foreign mail
and hits bottom with a sound
that tells me my letter is alone.
They will have to bring in a plane
from a place of coastline and beaches,
from a climate of fresh figs and apricot,
to cradle my one letter. Up in the air
it will leave behind some of its ugly nuance,
its unpleasant habit of humanity
which wants to smear itself over others:
the spot in which it wasn't clear, perhaps,
how to take my words, which were suggestive,
the paragraph in which the names of flowers,
ostensibly to indicate travel,
make a bed for lovers,
the parts that contain spit and phlegm,
the words only a wet tongue can manage,
hissing sounds and letters of the alphabet
which can only be formed
by biting down on the bottom lip.
In the next-to-last paragraph, some hair
came off in the comb. Then clothes
were gathered from everywhere in the room
in one sentence, and the sun rose
while a door closed with sincerity.
No doubt such sincerity will be judged,
but first the investigation of the postmark.
Am I where I was expected? Did I have at hand
the right denominations of stamps,
or did I make a childish quilt of ones and sevens?

Ah yes, they will have to cancel me twice.
Once to make my words worthless.
Once more to stop me from writing.

Late Naps

There is a dead part of the day
when the soul goes away—the late afternoon,
for me, or else why is it
that sleep starts up in the stomach
in the late afternoons? The feeling,
like blood thinning-out up and across a gray
lining of stomach and intestines,
leads through moral disquiet to anxiety
to metaphysical alarm and then
sublime terror. Was anyone ever so scared?
Maybe you as the reader of this poem
can tell me: why can't the things one put back,
what one left behind, gave up on
or failed, keep their curses to themselves?
How is it that they who stand dumb in dream
know just when we are weakest,
and come again with their *if only*'s? You
tell me, I only know the bed
and the window and the blankets. I only know
the right side of the alarm clock,
and the paper cigarettes of the magazines
in the slim hands of the hazardous models
I take to my two pillows.
I only know the grain of that thing
that turns over and over in the mind
while the day turns
smoothly into the absolute cobalt of night.
And this happens even though,
like you, I took steps.
I left the Goddess' lava where it was,
I took nothing from the tombs.
I sent regrets, I left well enough. . . .
I know the dreamworks run on an oil so light,
it can be distilled from thin air.
In dreams, the sun is just a lamp,

and the soul—the soul is laughable,
putting on bedsheets or hovering in a cloud
of anesthesia with the melancholy eyes
of a wealthy schoolboy.
Some say the soul doesn't like to be taken
out of the body. Perhaps they're right,
for it gets nervous when the light fails.
It doesn't like getting dressed or flying.
It would like to just lie down and sleep for once,
leaving the ulcers to proxies,
and not wake up for a while.

Someone Is Probably Dead

1

I already knew the secrets of light
before the snow.
It's the little light snowflakes—the dust,
not the pancakes—that make me crazy.
It's the little ones that make a blanket
of my coat and shut
out the stars and a chance to think.
Sometimes, there can be a blizzard where I stand
and nowhere else.
It's the same when a bright sun
in a hard sky
makes the plants in the window fuller.
I take it personally.
And even now, hiding from the snow,
just ten p.m., a Tuesday,
I sit under a green bursting indoors plant
with this feeling. The plant, surviving
nights I forgot to give it heat,
waterless weeks and a rough way
of doing business with it, all the time in its own way
picking off the red hairs of sunlight
and turning out succulent leaves that look like
skin on thick thumbs
or something worse—guts, maybe—manages. Doesn't
pilfer or make everyone around it miserable
against the day it will be picked up by one limp wing
and thrown down into the fly-infested trash.

2

Sometimes, I'll have been sick for three years,
but not with fever and thrashing
and the sheets torn round so that any doctor
would see at once a tight damp picture of illness.
No, sick with calm,

the catatonia of still beauty, the pretty prison
of memory, sometimes
just a face, just a name. It's a wonder
we're alive, we so much prefer the dead.

3
So once I took a ride in Chicago.
The cabbie's name was Purchase Slaughter.
He was all business. Not a star.
But a name that goes from here to there.
So I'm going to put him right here in front of you
and explain to you that when you drive
a taxi in the city for ten hours a day forever
you end up sitting perfectly still
and the city goes by you, turns right and left,
stops and starts up and you immobile
in your thoughts. Mr. Slaughter,
the anti-hero of these lines,
probably stands tonight in the snow off Lake Michigan
and curses the weather
which robs him of his income
and makes him live another life—or nothing.

4
It's stupid to pretend we can be someone else,
when someone else is dead.

Tired

1

The utter fatigue of the pebble
kicked loosely by every foot that passes.
The running joy in coming down
four hours back from Alaska.
The lost writing instrument.
The laundry in plastic.
The airliner magazine for its ads.
Four hours past but not yet lived.
To be done over if one chooses.
Not having seen a night in ten days.

The shirts with their arms behind them,
backs broken, wrinkled necks,
like something beheaded,
honorable once, still bearing
the stain of happiness,
the sweat, the wine and the hair.

Penny's yellow shirt: under
the red sun and caribou, "Alaska/
Our Last Chance," and it fits.
The late yellow light of Midnight Sun
in the cockpit and below
the spongy tundra, the silt-laden
faucets of the glaciers.
The white water of the brown Nenana.
The bluebells in the loose banks
and the wild rose the light flattens.
For there was a spreading there
like that of a face pushed against light—
whether the face of a red flower, or evergreen,
or of the visitor, feeling at home.

2

He goes. Through forty hours of daylight
he is hurried toward darkness.
He sits on the right side of the airplane,
looks over his shoulder, and thinks:

Let's have some dirt in the teeth,
the blue moon of the famous song,
an anthem for the coach class,
something!, something! This high-flying hush
is for sleeping. And sleeping
is for forgetting.

Letters from Africa

The self is small, and growing smaller.
But I write only: How are the children?
Every other day, in the morning,
while it is still the middle of the night for them,
I tell them I have awoken feeling fine.
By the time they read it, I may be ill,
sick as a bony Moroccan dog
from a germ so utterly common,
it needs no name.

But this moment I am well,
which makes me think they too are well,
and in six hours will also rise
and send their greetings also: *feeling fine*.
It is easier to write to them
if I imagine them awake.

Still, they sleep.
They do not hear my typing,
nor the sadness in my salutation:
Dear, uttered to three who sleep.
While there is time to decide what to write.

Does it matter that I looked for a letter,
that I have found a bookstore,
that I have changed my address? Or how the boys
felt four days ago across the ocean?
That it rains, and stops raining,
and rains again and the winds change direction?
No sails will bring my letters.
Will the date I put at the top matter
if we stay married? If we do not?

I place on a bench a bath towel, folded,
and the bench I place on a thick rug,

and the typewriter on the towel,
and I sit on the bed's edge and drink coffee
and write home, and never look up.
I have no view anyway. My window opens to
shutters, and the shutters to a stone wall,
white of course, with a lit window no one passes
though a bottle of water waits
half-empty on a small balcony. Why curtains
in a room with no view?
Dutifully, I open them mornings
and close them nights and at intimate moments,
to no end. No one can see, it seems
there is no one here who might want to,
no one who knows me knows that I am here,
and no one who sees me will know that it is I.

Yet if only because of this day,
I must think more about the light
that enters a room with no view,
and what I think is this:
As the light is no view, but better,
I am not here in this small room
and in these small details,
but abroad in the hearts of others,
even in other times
when I may have ceased to exist
but the last letter arrives without knowing.

Let me live now in the world without knowing.
The mustard grasses shine like thousands
of suns. The eucalyptus is statelier than I.
What good is it to be away
and not want to go home?

During the War

I was one of those who sees something cross the moon
and is never again the same person.
I was one of those who fought for an envelope, for a stamp.
I was one who felt the pain of the potted plant
and the loneliness of the tree.

It was all in my mind. It was an idea I had!
Was it such a bad idea?
Did it hurt anyone? Did it even delay for a minute
a father thousands of miles from me
fleeing a tank from my own beloved country?

Did it hasten the deaths by bombing?
Did it quicken the suffering of the homeless?

Certainly not. Absolutely, unequivocally, the answer is No.
My love for the tree did not interfere
with one decision of a committee, one staff meeting.
My joining forces with the mysterious
did not blot a single marching order, nor break a rifle.

The world went on without me. To its mind,
I was no part of it, but to my mind I was too much a part.
I put it all down on paper but in code.
Even at night, I watched the skies like a spy
for the intersection of a planet and the future.

2

You Can Keep the Sun Out of Your Eyes with Just One Hand

Here I am, in the 1950s,
giving up on Literature.
There's been a heart attack,
a sort of kidnapping
in the family, a near-drowning,
several fishermen lost
on the edge of a hurricane,
and an astonishing change-over
of roles when a girl I know
becomes her son's big sister
and gets a chance to start over.
The kid's wise to everything
but his sister (his mother)
and his mother (grandmother),
and a smudgy cloud of convenience
descends on the legal papers.
I'm young in all this
but don't forget, and someday
as a radioman will copy
sixty words-per-minute of continuous
wave which, for their telegraphic
style, could be messages from Hemingway,
a famous hunter and suicide.
Like him, I become a newspaper
hack, writing filler
and going out in the vicious part
of winter nights to
be there when the body is named
and beat the obit. deadline.
Gone at 2 in the morning to a lake
where my once-best teacher
has taken his life, and I have a story
to get in, his notes
making good sense about why

except that the word Buddha and another one,
Christ, make the policemen uncomfortable—
I know by now that art
is a part of life, and I know which part
it is. Because,
I wouldn't lay a poem down
to cover a drowned man's bloated face,
a huge abscess really,
waiting to be drained and that's all.
I would hope to hell
not to cover my tracks with elegies,
or ever to break the news
that was hidden to save harm.
There are some people best left
nailed to their secrets. Once,
in Hemingway's *corrida* haunt,
I saw a bull drop dead untouched,
humiliating the matador,
probably by choice, and certainly
for good reason.

Cuba, Fifties

I'm a teenager in a towel
and the government is falling.
In the hallway, two brownshirts
are breaking down a door . . .
and a man is taken, while I
stand in a small towel
to put in order the machine gun
in the street, a scared cabbie,
the girl who put the coins
into my friend's hand and signalled
a slow cop, and now this.
I go back to my room
and tell the girl to go with God.
I have to tell my friend
through the door of his room
three times to get going,
and no wonder when I see the beauty
he's been trying to position.
There isn't time for love
or even rum, which we've a case of
to give to the road crew
by the airport. No time
to look for the three Canadians
who knew the hotel. They
may be gone already, who else
would hitch the Keys
to fly to Havana
to be caught distracted in a revolution
wearing only a towel?
I can't be stupid enough
to earn these moments,
I tell myself, but I am. In Miami
it's all over—the slow news
from the island will pump up
the cigar trade for a while.

In the half-open but air-conditioned
stand-up bar, a man takes my hot
cigarette, touches it to
his arm, his armpit and his neck.
Puffs it up again, this time
to his tongue, chews it and swallows.
It's a stupid trick that burns him,
but we talk for hours.

He Said To

crawl *toward* the machine guns
except to freeze
for explosions and flares.
It was still ninety degrees
at night in North Carolina,
August, rain and all.
The tracer bullets wanted
our asses, which we swore to keep
down, and the highlight
of this preposterous exercise
was finding myself in mud
and water during flares. I
hurried in the darkness—
over things and under things—
to reach the next black pool
in time, and once
I lay in the cool salve that
so suited all I had become
for two light-ups of the sky.
I took one inside and one
face of two watches I ruined
doing things like that,
and made a watch that works.
From the combat
infiltration course and
common sense, I made a man
to survive the Army, which means
that I made a man to survive
being a man.

In America

these things happen: I am taken
to see a friend
who talks too fast and is now teaching *Moby Dick*
according to jujitsu,
or judo according to Melville:
He says Melville gets you leaning
and lets go, or gets you to pulling
and suddenly advances, retreats
when you respond, and so on. Ok, I
accept that, but then he starts
in on the assassination of
John F. Kennedy as planned by our
government, and he has a collection of
strange deaths at handy times
bizarrely of people who know something.
I know nothing. I want to know
nothing whatsoever. It once
was enough to be standing
on a field of American baseball,
minding my ground balls and business,
when the infielder to my left
shot me the news of what is now known as
The Bay of Pigs, then in progress
but secretly, and certainly
doomed for stupidity, mis-timing,
marsh-landings, and JFK's resolve
to unaccomplish the Agency's *fait accompli*
by refusing air cover. This would crackle
the air waves, but later. Tall tales,
I figured, wrongly,
putting my fist in my glove
for America.
Moby Dick, you damn whale,
I've seen whales.
America, though—
too big to be seen.

The Mummies of Guanajuato

For a peso,
the dead men at corridor's end
will fight for the girl
between them, and one
will die fighting, the girl
from grief and the last one
from stupidity. Fortunately,
my Spanish stinks, the kid
talks without emotion,
and the whole experience lacks
form except for the clammy hall
underground where they stand.
The kid's background
probably moves to the girl
from whose wrist hangs a fetus
by a wire, and to the ones with hair
like hair and nails like nails
and unblinking sockets.
I stare into the hall of bones
where those who were too poor
to stay buried, but got
a year, now get eternity.
Dug up to make room,
some of them were worth more dead
than they had hoped,
but it costs nothing to see them
if you don't mind the drop
down the sewer hole in the damp,
and a peso for the kid
to tell his story and keep
the other kids from telling theirs.

On and On

We tried to close
the 24-hour Café de Paris
by telling long stories.
From the walls of photos,
soccer stars starred—
dribbling or tackling
or performing the incredible
scissor-kick over one's head
for the goal-of-the-year.
My friend reported a king snake
in the zoo
who moved. It took him
two liqueurs and a beer
to get the moving snake
to catch itself
and go back to sleep.
There was a polar story
too, in which a bear
ran in the Arctic—
I believe my friend
and the pilot were all
who saw it. A reference
might have been made
to the crowds at the cage
of the bull elephant
in the St. Louis Zoo
of natural causes.
I had that afternoon
seen the moving picture,
"Children of Paradise,"
and now I knew why many
returned to it from a distance.
She who went in a carriage
while the crowd closed forever
on her lover—her story

and his, that had so often
continued, would now stop
without an ending,
and only the emotions
of loss and sadness
and the utter depth of life
which offers us no footing
would go on. Therefore,
when my turn came
in the Café, I told
the plot, but not the story.
It would have had
a terrible effect
among the animals and athletes—
the still snake,
the sluggish bear,
and the impotent bull elephant—
to exhibit the strange case of humanity,
whose suffering goes on and on.

Some Shadows

On the snow at night,
I saw once the shadow
of a huge sound,
which I had heard begin
as I passed under an old cherry tree,
then immaculate for winter.
There was the preparation,
which I can only say I heard,
though sound came next.
There was the sound, all at once—
a living thing, lifting.
I felt a giant presence
and looked down.
When I looked up, the shadow
I had seen leaving
took all the sky.
Too big for me,
I thought, but when I thought again
I could see again the owl
I had seen on the lawn of the church
the morning the Methodists
met to make the softball team.
Over its head, it wore
a number 3 paper bag.
Someone thought it could see better
in the dark. It
spoke a little, took a step
this way and that,
before someone else put it under an arm
and took it toward dusk.
I walked on the lawn
with the good Boy Scouts, thinking,
that dumb owl. Come out in the open
like that. I can see him today,
slowed by sunlight,

stuck to his shadow.
Inside the paper bag,
his pinned wing
made a sound like applause.

We Had Seen a Pig

1

One man held the huge pig down
and the other stuck an icepick
into the jugular, which is when
we started to pay attention.
The blood rose ten feet with force
while the sow swam on its back
as if to cut its own neck.
Its fatty back smacked the slippery
cement while the assassins shuffled
to keep their balance, and the bloody
fountain rose and fell back and rose
less and less high, until
the red plume re-entered the pig
at the neck, and the belly collapsed
and the pig face went dull.

2

I knew the pig
was the butcher's, whose game
lived mainly behind our garage.
Sometimes turkeys, always
roosters and sheep. Once the windmill
turned two days without stopping.
The butcher would walk in his apron
straight for the victim. The others
would scratch and babble
and get in the way.
Then the butcher would lead the animal
to the back door of his shop,
stopping to kill it on a stump.
It was always evening, after closing.
The sea breeze would be rising,
cloaking the hour in brine.

3

The pig we saw slaughtered
was more than twice anything
shut up in the patch
we trespassed to make havoc.
Since the butcher was Italian,
not Jewish, that would be his pig.
Like the barber who carried
a cigar box of bets
to the stationery store, like
the Greek who made sweets
and hid Greek illegals,
immigrant "submarines,"
the butcher had a business, his
business, by which he took
from our hands the cleaver and serrated
knife for the guts,
and gave us back in butcher paper
and outer layers of brown wrapping
our lives for their cries.

4

Hung up to drain, the great pig,
hacked into portions,
looked like a puzzle
we could put together in the freezer
to make a picture of
a pig of course, a map, clothes or other things
when we looked.

Things I Took

The back shell of a crab.
Stones from the sea.
A feather and a duck's foot.
Too much thought about childhood.
Too many pictures
of my home town. The umbrella
the Union Avenue oaks made
down to the dock at the Bay.
The Little Dipper, easy to see.
The blown seeds of the dandelion,
the grass whistles,
the propellors weeds made,
the tests of flowers (love
and butter), the inks of berries.
And much more,
light as these things were.

Now they are back in place,
I can tell you
why I drove to Westhampton,
nearest the ocean,
the day of the hurricane.
From Bellport, I had seen the Atlantic
lapping Fire Island's
thinnest strip, where stilts
held up the houses while the dunes
moved inches for miles.
I hurried to cross a bridge
toward fury. That was my job.
Others were shuttering windows,
bringing in boats or just loosening
the ties and running. In 1938,
a storm brought some of Florida
to New York, and boats down Union,

trees down in the schoolyard
and enough mud and brine to pack a town in.

So much self!
Look at stanza one
compared to stanza two—the things
themselves, their specific
densities, differ. You can see
for yourself in what you remember
the place where strength of spirit
begins, the loss of words, etc.
For the soul doesn't call to itself,
nor is it locked in ice
when the water freezes, nor transported
by rushing water, unless the one
who watches watches by holding still.
In the wind, the soul is not always moving.
In the calm, the soul may not be.
Compare stanza one to stanza two.
Much more could have gone into the one,
nothing of consequence
into the other. I got as close
as I could before the waves
raked up enough of the ocean floor
to convince me.

That Time in Tangier

The world seemed smaller—
I could sense the globe's curving—
in Tangier, where the far end
was mountain and the mid-view sea.
If my letters got from there to here—
a colossal mission?, dumb luck?—
I got none back, only the wind
off the churlish Straits,
and Gibraltar, and pigeon pie.
In the medina, the chemists
made perfumes to tumble a goddess,
in the spice-seller's wooden tray
were the bowels of the earth,
and the water-sellers in their coats
of cups rattled their measures.
Lonely, I went to Trudy's
Viennese Piano Bar and there
one empty night, playing
her piano myself, found Trudy too
to be stuck there, refugee
from a war zone, who having saved
her life found it was not her life
she had saved, it wasn't there
to be run from or even gone home to.
I didn't want to be anyone so alone.
In my watch cap, beard and dark raincoat,
I went quickly past the hustlers
to the deep wells of the market
where tin slats corrugated the sunlight
and striped us like jailbirds.
Drumming from a street beyond
stopped me, and I knew I would end up
part of a band of those drummers,
hitting the small ones between my knees
and the larger ones beneath an arm,

hands and sticks and a flying raincoat,
probably a crazy man if the air
had not been drumbeats for whatever
festival, and as I say I knew
what language they spoke,
but just before that, as I turned
full in the path of the beating,
I lost my loneliness,
which was most of what I had brought
from home, and could have stayed.

The Canal at Rye

Don't let them tell you—
the women or the men—
they knew me.
You knew me.
Don't let them tell you
I didn't love your mother.
I loved her.
Or let them tell you.
Do you remember Rye?—
where the small fishing boats,
deprived of the receding sea,
took the tide out,
a canal so thin they had to go
single-file, sails of suns,
while the red sun rose.
That town was old.
A great novelist lived there.
Do you know him?
Not many will be reading
his long sentences.
And they are punished.
For that is *our* sentence: to be
dumb in a passage we think turns
from darkness to light
but doesn't. Turn back
to art, including the sentence.
It is also the world. Whoever understands
the sentence understands
his or her life. There are reasons
not to, reasons too
to believe or not to. But
reasons do not complete an argument.
The natural end and extension
of language

is nonsense. Yet there is safety
only there. That is why Mr. Henry James
wrote that way—
out with the tide, but further.

The Last Thing I Say

to a thirteen-year-old sleeping,
tone of an angel, breath of a soft wing,
I say through an upright dark space
as I narrow it pulling the door
sleepily to let the words go surely into
the bedroom until I close them in
for good, a nightwatchman's-worth
of grace and a promise for morning
not so far from some God's first notion
that the world be an image by first light
so much better than pictures of hope
drawn by firelight in ashes,
so much clearer too, a young person
wanting to be a man might draw one finger
along an edge of this world and it
would slice a mouth there
to speak blood and then should he put that wound
into the mouth of his face,
he will be kissed there and taste
the salt of his father as he lowers
himself from his son's high bedroom
in the heaven of his image of
a small part of himself and sweet dreams.

3

Benny Hooper

Now that I'm older,
Now that my legs show the blue veins
That crossed my country
Seven times at least, and the flowers
The needles left
Have wrinkled up and away under
Some implacable color of my darkening skin,
Now I can see things better.

The legs have to get lousy
And many tiny nerve-ends have to be burnt
Completely off
And the heart turn leathery
Before the brain is free,
And the eyes, a little
Duller, are better.

Who has a choice?

I don't fuss. Look at
What comes back. I
Haven't seen a potato
So closely in twenty-five years.
No, longer! I never saw one then,
Though there were more of them than rocks
In Mattituck.
They went underground to grow, and back
Underground to wait for the jobbers.
How many of you know
How many eyes of a potato
You can eat before you die?

Another underground story I can tell
Concerns the Hooper kid
Falling into the well. Doctor Kris,

That kind man, stayed
In the floodlights when the young newsmen
Were inside drinking coffee.
It took two nights and a day but they saved the kid.
After the hoopla of the press, the parents
Didn't know enough to thank the doc.
Now that's what comes from growing White
Potatoes in the dark. One day
You can't see nothing
Except underground.

A Motor

The heavy, wet, guttural
Small-plane engine
Fights for air, and goes down in humid darkness
About where the airport should be.
I take a lot for granted,
Not pleased to be living under the phlegm-
Soaked, gaseous, foggy and irradiated
Heavens whose angels wear collars in propjets
And live elsewhere in Clean Zones,
But figuring the air is full of sorrows.

I don't blame
The quick use of the entire earth
On the boozy
Pilot
Come down to get a dose of cobalt
For his cancer. He's got
A little life left, if
He doesn't have to take all day to reach it.
With the black patches
Inside him, and
The scars and the streaks and the sick stomach,

His life is more and more like
That of the lowliest child chimney sweep
In the mind of the great insensible,
William Blake. William Blake,
The repeated one, Blake, the half-mad,
Half-remembered,
Who knew his anatomy, down to
The little-observed muscle in the shoulder
That lifts the wing.

The little London chimney sweeper
Reaches up and reaches down.

In his back,
Every vertebra is separated from the long
Hours of stretching.
With one deep, tired breath,
The lungs go black.

By the Holiday Company crane,
Adding a level to the hospital,
On the highest land in the county,
Heavy sits the pure-white Air Care
Helicopter, with
Its bulging eye.
It has kept many going, a good buy,
Something.

Now someone I know says Blake
In anger,
Angry for his brother in the factory
And his sister on the ward,
But tonight I have no more anger
Than the muscle
That lifts my knee when I walk.

Another pleads with the ocean
That the words for
Suffering and trouble
Take place in a sound that will be all sounds
And in the tidal roll
Of all our lives and every event,
But I am silent by water,
And am less to such power
Than a failed lung.

And I think it is only a clever trick to know
That one thing may be contained

In another. Hence,
Blake in the sweep, one in the ground
In one in the air,
Myself in the clinic for runaway cells,
Now and later.

Birds Who Nest in the Garage

God keeps his oath to sparrows
Who of little love know how to starve.

Emily Dickinson

1

I'm coming, clear out. They shit
on the bulb in the lamp on the ceiling
until the light emerges weakly
like an old man's flashlight through spit
in the frozen, icy ground in deepest winter
where ten months ago
he was buried alive
with his wonderful American life-long batteries.
I'm coming, get moving.
A nice life, alright, nesting on a light fixture
for two years now, and the second season
discovering the side mirror
and the joy of seeing yourselves, first the feathered
fright, then the calm power
pecking and shitting, pecking and shitting.
Everyone knows my car by now.

I'm coming, get out there in the spring,
out in the rain that's coming.
What do you think you birds are for anyway?

2

People tell me things. I can tell when they want to.
There were these two young men, boys,
running, and one carried a laundry bag or something,
a ruggedness to them and a raggedness
to the way they ran, cars
having to stop short, etc., and from in between
parked cars a girl appeared and waited for me
to pass, leaning a little.
A long face and long coat, off-white skin

like the pure white of new snow under clouds,
yellow slacks the color of cheap paper,
and huge eyes getting larger,
something to say to me, maybe, but first
I had to make sure. It was her life.
And in the mirror, veering the car as I drove past
to get an angle, again that crusty
white of well-fed swifts and swallows,
and feathers too, brown edges of their fights all
against themselves, and
the brownest markings of old blood.
Let the girl go. She'll be young tomorrow.
Can't the birds sing, though?
You'd think that, if they listened to themselves at all,
they'd be happy.

3
Something the same
can be said for the owl and dove
who hoot their blacks and grays
night and morning. The dove's the one—
too-hoo too-hoo—who mourns but
with clear pleasure. He wakes us.
He can't be sad enough!
The owl, though: a *whoot-whoot*
like the claws of an intellectual.
He is happy too, at night
when he eats.

Mornings, *too-hoo*.
Nights, *whoot-whoot*.

That leaves the days and dusk
to the littlest,
the ones that hide,

the ones that cover the light
by moving in dark bunches,
the ones through whom spring moves
with a commotion of branches
and who cover my car
with the pulp of my own wild cherries
and the shell of the ladybug
and the hair of the legs of flies
and a glue and a paste
and—who knows?—a balm and a salve.

Probably there's someone somewhere
who could tell you
if you're good enough friends,
and if you were feeling small that day,
that not enough attention is paid
to what the birds do.

They die in bunches.
They build their homes on the edges,
the beams and eaves
blistered and crusted by what they let go
in several lifetimes.

Also, the proof is everywhere:
they can't eat enough.
Lord knows, they try.

A dust of feathers.
Soon no more.

A Shrug

Let's see,
if I have it right,
the statue of Balzac that stands in Paris
resembling a tree, all feelingly
up from its roots (feet) like an *old* tree,
gnarled and corrugated—
this statue was damned because it looked too much
like a tree, all feelingly
up sexually, all outdoors-like, seemingly
open to anything,
maybe under his stone coat the great Balzac
is masturbating,
which gives his face the flush look
of its character
where the rain rains red
and the waiters push the young café crowd
out to linger in the rain for free.

You don't believe the rain is red?
Go and look.
Good dirt is always partly blue
and city rain is red.
It's a scandal that we continue
to speak of our water as clear
when we can see it in the air,
and to speak of our ideas
as inviolable ideals. The world can stuff our mouths
with the opaqueness of life
and violation.

I had a moment near Balzac in Paris
which I treasure.
A corner boy, one of those Left Bank schoolboys
who feed heavy jellied candies
to the coach class who empty mid-evenings

from the jittery budget hotels
on *Rue des Écoles*,
and from whom I bought something sticky,
palmed the better part of my change
and handed me the small bills only,
while he chattered like a host
of his great love for Americans.
This is a game I happen to know
to watch for when the talk turns Balzacian.
When I turned, he was ready
with my money, and a good smile in the silence.

Let's see,
if I have it right,
Rodin's *Balzac* was thought too rough, obscene,
and of course it was intended that way,
as if to keep something from you
until you want it,
and then to give it all to you with a shrug.

What's the matter?
You don't believe the rain in Paris is red?

At the Airport

1

If it happened to you,
maybe you wouldn't know what to say.

The snow drips for hours
while you are inside having coffee
and when your friend has carefully climbed
into the belly of the plane,
while hoses play along the wings to break up
ice and give the plane a knife's chance,
has willingly gone to where
the coffee is now,
and with twenty-five like-minded salesmen
for one thing and another,
and twenty-five portfolios,
one or two grandparents
and the rest half-grown college students
going home, has risen
into one of those holes that opens for a moment
in a sky that is wet cloth,
you breach the freezing air again
and you are like a man wearing the night before for a coat
who seems to be perfectly ok
like anyone
covered by the snow.
But you know.

2

Earlier, I watched the coffee making
and the smell of the roast
undid the weather and undid too
the salts that settle in sleep
and stirred the heavy metals and made, also,
the eyelids light

and the eyes baffled and the eyelids blown open
to make it out to be the day.

Paltry, our words for smells—
this one *like this* and this one *like that*,
but the eye follows.
Near the airport, the smell that broke in
upon us was that of burnt cereal—
from the Quaker Oats chimneys in Cedar Rapids,
forced down and spread out by the snow.
The new people—the ones whose friends say,
"They've gone to see the Rapids"—
pay plenty to live windward of the stacks.

Downwind, where the Czechs have always lived,
and the Oats workers,
the smell's another thing:
not a curtain but a blanket, a cash equivalent
against the cold.
Nobody had to tell them
they were going to get their noses dirty
and maybe they wouldn't like it!

3
I have gone past
farms rolling back from the highway
black with the shit of pigs,
and have driven through the yellow mud
the cart drops
between the barn on one side of the road
and the field on the other,
the squeezed pulp of the insides of pigs
who have had all they could eat,
and the dark smell
has raised the organs in my throat

until I could not speak to swear. Goddammit,
people have to live here.

And I—I have to use this paper
that smelled in, say, Missoula, Montana
or somewhere in the logging woods
like a leaf,
and then in, say, Missoula, Montana
or elsewhere in a paper milling company town,
stunk the acrid smell of crushed
veins, the pulpy stench of burnt skin,
the yellow smell of hands,
this nothing paper, this once-raggy, over-
laundered excuse for paper,
not smelling even of linen, perfect
for the rain.

4
So my friend gets on and goes
all day in the metal blister of a DC-10,
resting his corridors of sense,
gorging on coffee,
and if he's lucky he lands in a dry place.
I go out to the surprising accumulation.
The snow is just water.
The poem is just paper. Unless

I say it's not.

Where Is Odysseus From and What Was He Before He Left for the Trojan War?

By a city building in Málaga—
upon a hill it was, but nothing important
had taken place or was taking place,
even inside us,
when we visited most of that year the five countries
in which the dollar was slipping
and fewer foreigners were tipping—
I found a pod that resembles
two shells of brown turtles,
hinged at one end, yawning at the other,
from which there escaped the tiniest wooden seeds
borne by the thinnest flakes of wings,
and no one there could say
what it was. So I took six.

On the brightest day, when I might have seen
a mermaid in the Mediterranean,
I saw the way the color changes
halfway out to the limits of particular vision.
It was green "here" and blue "out there."
It was sky-blue, where blue.
It was a put-up green, where green, a made
green, a vegetable green.

How could I know much?
I hadn't been there a year.
I had yet to say a single thing clearly
in the language.
I hadn't seen inside my shoulders
where they hurt for some reason.
I couldn't see behind me and go forward,
but I kept looking back.

It became a matter of a gummy substance
I scraped from a tree,

a matter of brittle y's of turtle-pods,
an importance of winged seeds,
an absolute blindness we see much of—
that takes the form most of all
of a love of nature.

No one has said this.

Five years later, I found again the turtle-pod
on a sub-tropical island,
and again no one could name it.
Again, I brought home three. Again,
I made a connection, I reached.

Yet
from every elsewhere,
we returned. From
the amazing propellor the guard wove
from a single weed
in sight of the gypsy caves of Granada.
From the fingers of broom,
the fields of mustard and gorse,
the England that hugs the hedges in Rye,
from the weight of stone that throws
itself into the water
at the far tip of Long Island
to best England,
and from far and away beyond our own language,
from Spain, from France, from Scotland,
and also from Morocco
that year.

It was our first trip abroad,
and we were thing-conscious. Oh, even to
Volubulis, a Greek city raised

from the centuries
to be ruins. While a wind rose
that could lift a jacket from a chair back,
and whitecaps moved north
to where Shelley stayed in 1812,
to where Wordsworth lived after he had lost it,
to where land begins and land ends.

It did not cease to be difficult.
The time it took to learn
from the many effects of travel
would be a long time,
like the time it takes a robin
in a dry spring full of enemies
to find and return with
a berry to soak and chew and then pass
from one mouth to another
in an instant.

We have not seen so much
that we may make of the woods a violin
to be played by the wind
while men must cure themselves.
Is there among us
one who can go anywhere
without looting or looking for ivory,
but advance the plot?

I renounce the souvenir,
the colorful photo, the clean stones and the pressed
leaves, the pods and the sponges.
I renounce the brass African sugar hammer
used by no one, the washed shells
emptied of life.

I shall keep the wide-bladed
pasta shears
because they made our supper
in Catalonia.

What They Do to You in Distant Places

I never told you.
There was a woman—in the greening season
of a tropical island
where I had gone to break some hard thoughts
across my knee
and also, although I am no athlete
but breathe with my stomach like the satyr
and live in my stomach
according to bile and acid and bread and bitter chocolate,
to run a long race for the first time.
On that morning,
it was raining in great screens
of the purest water and almost no one at 4 a.m.
where I waited, half-sheltered
by the edge of my dark hotel, for a let-up.
Except her, suddenly
from nowhere—smelling of long hair and dew,
smelling of dew and grass and a little powder.
She wore a dress that moved.
She had been out dancing and the night and she
were young.
I wore a black watch cap like an old sailor
but I was all there was.

I said no, I had to do something else.
She asked how far? And
if I would run all that way—hours.
I said I'd try,
and then she kissed me for luck
and her mouth on mine was as sweet as the wild guava
and the smell of her hair
was that of the little bit of dew the lover
brings home from the park
when again she shows up in the morning.

I don't know where I have been
that I have ever had such a kiss
that asked nothing and gave everything.
I walked out into the rain
as if blessed. But I had forgotten
what they do to you in distant places,
taking away your memory
before sending you back. You and me.
I confess,
I forgot her within the hour
in the gross odors of my labors.
If I had known what she was doing. . . .
Perhaps she's with you now.

Italian

It would be enough
if Marvin, on his first scared journey
to Italy,
found there in the gassy rainbows
in puddles in the gear-stripped, tarred,
broken, bled on and often washed
streets of Rome
a sky to go home in. He must be
looking for something—
this child of an island—
to have crossed the ocean and Alps
without gold, without
one book on birds or plants. God,
how he hopes he hasn't come
just for a self-portrait.
So in the gassy air with green pears
and the arc of a banana
left from a pocket's lunch
leading him on. He has a habit of bananas
and of not peeling them in time.
They point at his feet and grow dark.
They are wasted.
But, if it comes to that,
they are not more wasted than marble,
which seems to have been used mainly
to break the people's backs
and interrupt the sun
and find another use for sand.
The air there could make you remember
a drawling sea,
or corn gone ripe into colors
and gathered for the holidays. He won't
want to stay by himself.
He won't be satisfied to make tiny flowers of type
alone in the hotel or café.

He won't be made beautiful by the news
of our dancing. No,
he wants to know which word means really.
He wants to know which word tells where two streets meet,
which word means turning around fast.
He wants to know which word means not tied.
And which means frightening.
He needs to know which word means an outside covering
on a house, and which one means
you think something happened.
He wants to know how long the growing season is.
At home. Once he put a hand
into the water somewhere in a flat wintry light
and the whitefish were the bones of diamonds,
so why not anyone?

Florence

Sure,
I could take back my life,
but how many stones would I have to carry in my pockets,
and these stones can't write their way
out of a paper bag!

This *pensione* stands near where Dante
first saw Beatrice, and now every trucker in town
uses the nearby bridge
in the hope of a glimpse.

How far back?

At the Kandinsky exhibit, I must have been mistaken
for an expatriate subversive.
The Russian guard followed me, studied me as I wrote
in front of Kandinsky's in-leaning "Red Square."

I endure, here,
the same craziness from not being able to speak
that made Kandinsky Kandinsky,
and makes the babbling pigeon lady of San Marco Square
talk to a mop,
and the bad teacher put words into the student's mouth.

But I'll tell you something.

Antonio Bonomo grows bananas to make your mouth water.
On the ceiling of the Sistine Chapel, Michelangelo's Jonah
is bigger than God.
And when Paolo Caliari Detto il Veronese
painted *The Last Supper* with dwarfs, dogs, Germans and spit
and was ordered to cover the blasphemy,
he simply changed the title

to *Feast at the House of Levi*. Now he's damned
for sure.

If you need to know why the air here
is never still, or if you bear
a philosophical bent of mind
or you are crippled by travel, or ill or bedraggled,
you will want to be told that the Levites
were the priests and, when the twelve tribes scattered,
they too went into hiding,
among you.

To an Adolescent Weeping Willow

I don't know what you think you're doing,
sweeping the ground. You
do it so easily, backhanded, forehanded.
You hardly bend. Really, you sway.
What can it mean
when a thing is so easy?

I threw dirt on my father's floor.
Not dirt, but a chopped green
dirt which picked up dirt.

I pushed the pushbroom.
I oiled the wooden floor of the store.

He bent over and lifted the coal
into the coalstove. With the back of the shovel
he came down on the rat just topping the bin
and into the fire.

What do you think? —Did he sway?
Did he kiss a rock for luck?
Did he soak up water
and climb into light and turn and turn?

Did he weep and weep in the yard?

Yes, I think he did. Yes,
now I think he did.

So, Willow, you come sweep my floor.
I have no store.
I have a yard. A big yard.

I have a song to weep.
I have a cry.

You who rose up from the dirt,
because I put you there
and like to walk my head in under
your earliest feathery branches—
what can it mean
when a thing is so easy?

It means you are a boy.

These Green-Going-to-Yellow

This year,
I'm raising the emotional ante,
putting my face
in the leaves to be stepped on,
seeing myself among them, that is;
that is, likening
leaf-vein to artery, leaf to flesh,
the passage of a leaf in autumn
to the passage of autumn,
branch-tip and winter spaces
to possibilities, and possibility
to God. Even on East 61st Street
in the blowzy city of New York,
someone has planted a gingko
because it has leaves like fans like hands,
hand-leaves, and sex. Those lovely
Chinese hands on the sidewalks
so far from delicacy
or even, perhaps, another gender of gingko—
do we see them?
No one ever treated us so gently
as these green-going-to-yellow hands
fanned out where we walk.
No one ever fell down so quietly
and lay where we would look
when we were tired or embarrassed,
or so bowed down by humanity
that we had to watch out lest our shoes stumble,
and looked down not to look up
until something looked like parts of people
where we were walking. We have no
experience to make us see the gingko
or any other tree,
and, in our admiration for whatever grows tall

and outlives us,
we look away, or look at the middles of things,
which would not be our way
if we truly thought we were gods.

Marvin Bell

Marvin Bell was born August 3, 1937 in New
York City, and grew up in Center Moriches, on
the south shore of eastern Long Island. He now
lives in Iowa City, where he teaches for The
University of Iowa. For his poetry he has received
the Lamont Award of The Academy of American
Poets, the Bess Hokin Award from *Poetry*, an
Emily Clark Balch Prize from *The Virginia
Quarterly Review* and fellowships from the
Guggenheim Foundation and the National
Endowment for the Arts. *Stars Which See, Stars
Which Do Not See* (1977) was a finalist for
the National Book Awards.